MOUNTAIN
BIKE
TECHNIQUES

MOUNTAIN BIKE TECHNIQUES

▲

An
Illustrated
Guide

▼

Dennis Coello
and
Ed Chauner

Lyons & Burford, Publishers

Interior Design by Howard P. Johnson

Printed in the United States of America

10 9 8 7 6 5 4 3 2

Library of Congress Cataloging-in-Publication Data

Coello, Dennis.
    Mountain bike techniques / Dennis Coello and Ed Chauner.
       p.   cm.
    ISBN 1-55821-193-4
    1. All-terrain cycling. I. Chauner, Ed, 1957– . II. Title.
GV1056.C64 1992
796.6—dc20
                                  92-26217
                                    CIP

CONTENTS

PREFACE

This book has a single purpose: to teach you, quickly and simply, how to ride a mountain bike. So it's just for beginners, right? *Wrong.* Although it is true that newcomers to the sport might benefit most from a careful study of what follows, all but the experts will find this book useful in learning better techniques and *unlearning* bad ones.

Think for a moment how most people learn to ride mountain bikes. They buy or borrow one, head into the hills with friends, and try to copy what their more experienced friends do to jump obstacles, take steep climbs, and keep from killing themselves on nasty descents. And that's great, if your friends are expert riders—and expert instructors. And if you can remember all the intricate moves and how to repeat them the first time you head out by yourself.

Mountain Bike Techniques is an alternative to this usual manner of learning how to have fun on fat tires. Ed Chauner is an expert mountain biker who makes his living teaching people how to ride and ski in the Rockies. Through photos and clear, concise instructions you will take Ed's class, step by step. An engineer by training, but a natural teacher and athlete, Ed brings together an understanding of both the physics and the physical demands of mountain biking, and makes both seem easy.

In one chapter I discuss riding techniques I've learned during my years of fully loaded backcountry touring here and abroad. In another I provide the defensive moves that have kept me alive while mountain biking in America's urban jungles. You will also learn how to handle those mechanical breakdowns most common to trail riders and how to get along with fellow trail users. This, plus the photography and my attempts throughout to convey in print all that Ed Chauner provides to his students in person, is my contribution to the project. But the expertise in riding and instruction and therefore, in essence, this book, are all Ed's.

Dennis Coello

1

INTRODUCTION TO THE MOUNTAIN BIKE

No, we're not going to begin with an analysis of frame angles and fork rake. This is a how-to-ride, not how-to-buy book. Nevertheless, now is the time for you to give your bike a very close look. Once you're in the saddle, learning the nuances of bike movement, your mind will be too busy to think about such things as which brake stops which wheel and how to lift or drop your chain a cog or two.

So take this book over to your bike and begin by flipping your brake levers, one at a time. Follow the individual cable that runs from lever to brake pad and note the brake/wheel relationship. That is, note which brake lever operates which wheel. Now do the same with the gear cables; trace each shift lever cable to the derailleur it operates.

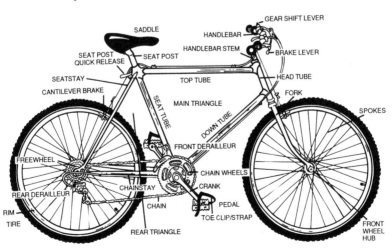

You'll find that the right-hand brake lever controls the rear-wheel brake, and the right-hand gear shift lever controls the rear-wheel derailleur. Etch this fact into your brain by repeating several times RIGHT REAR, RIGHT REAR, RIGHT REAR. Go ahead, say it—out loud. You'll remember it better, even if you do feel a bit silly talking to yourself.

Next, we'll adjust the saddle and handlebar height. Straddle the bike. Lift yourself into the saddle (this will be easier when bracing yourself in a doorway or against a wall) and place the *heel* of one foot on the pedal spindle (the axle, or middle of the pedal). Rotate this pedal to its bottom-of-the stroke (six o'clock) position, then raise or lower the saddle (by tripping the seatpost quick-release skewer) until your leg is fully extended. When riding, only the ball of your foot should be on the pedal. This heel fitting technique will therefore cause the leg to be slightly bent at full downstroke, a good beginning saddle height for most riding situations.

Now raise or lower your handlebars until they are almost even with, or slightly below, your saddle. Once again, you might want to alter the height later, but this is a good place to start. Pavement and touring mountain bikers generally prefer their bars almost even with the saddle; trail riders most often drop theirs an inch or so lower.

· **Determining saddle height** ·

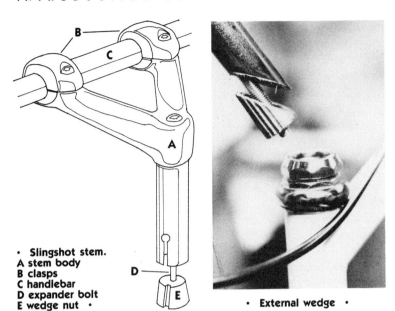

· Slingshot stem.
A **stem body**
B **clasps**
C **handlebar**
D **expander bolt**
E **wedge nut ·**

· **External wedge** ·

But raising or lowering your handlebars is easier said than done, because there's no seatpost-like quick-release skewer for the bars. The following paragraphs, borrowed from *The Mountain Bike Repair Handbook* (New York: Lyons & Burford, 1990), might help.

First, raising and lowering your handlebars does not involve the headset, so do not begin messing with the stack of locknuts and lockwashers immediately above your head tube. All that is involved is an expander bolt and wedge nut, an understanding of how things work in this part of the bike, and a few good wallops in the right place.

Notice the expander bolt in the drawing. At the other end of this bolt—inside the head tube—is either an angle-expander nut (see photo) or a wedge nut (an exterior or interior wedge). When the expander bolt is tightened, the angled nut presses against the head-tube wall; the wedge-nut type works by drawing the nut up inside the stem, forcing the stem walls against the head tube.

Now take the second important step in all mechanical repairs: a *close* look at everything that might be affected or at all involved. In the case of lowering or raising bars, your brake assembly may be involved (through the lengthening or shortening of the brake cable). If this is so with your bike, simply disengage the brake cable until the handlebar is adjusted, then readjust the cable length and reattach it when you're through.

Loosen the expander bolt two or three turns. You will notice when it becomes easier to turn. Try not to back it out from the bolt entirely; if you do, you'll then have to turn your bike upside down to free the nut. If your bike is new your bars can probably be moved when the expander bolt is loosened. But if not you'll have to rap the top of the expander bolt when it is loosened but still connected to the frozen angle or wedge nut inside the head tube. Use a mallet, the backside of a crescent wrench, or anything appropriate or nearby. You'll feel it release inside. Position the bars where you wish and retighten the expander bolt.

You're ready to saddle up, but before you do, it is important to think about *where* to practice your riding technique. You're probably anxious to hit the trails, but that's no place to learn the basics.

Physical skills are learned most efficiently when each new technique can be studied by itself—that is, when all other things remain the same and you can concentrate exclusively on the new maneuver. Those who teach skiing and biking and other sports call this procedure of adding only one new skill at a time the establishment of a "comfortable learning environment."

For example, let's say you want to learn how to swim. Your instructor would not suggest that you walk to the end of the diving board, leap into the middle of the pool, and attempt to backstroke to safety. Obviously the distracting, discomforting (and dangerous) variables of the diving board and deep end of the pool should be jettisoned. A far more comfortable learning environment, leading to more success in learning to swim, would be attained by slowly walking into the water at the shallow end.

Try to keep this example in mind as you progress through the skill levels in mountain biking. Because everyone reading this book can already ride a bike, and because ATBs (all-terrain bikes, another name for mountain bikes) are so much easier to ride than the relatively skittish touring and sport-racing bikes, the tendency is to head into the hills on backcountry trails long before you've learned the techniques necessary for safe and enjoyable travel.

In short, be patient and keep your comfort zone in mind. Change only one variable (the riding surface of pavement, dirt, gravel, or rocks; the steepness of your path; the technique being learned) at a time. An appropriate learning environment will be recommended for each skill.

SHIFTING

SHIFT LEVERS

Mountain bike shift levers are usually found in one of two places—above or below the handlebars. If you have under-the-bar levers you will notice that one lever is larger than the other. This

larger lever will shift your chain to a larger sprocket; the smaller lever will shift it to a smaller sprocket. So here's another mantra for you: LARGE LEVER, LARGE SPROCKET; SMALL LEVER, SMALL SPROCKET.

So much for the tough mental work. Now let's concentrate on how shift lever movement correlates with what your legs feel. First, the right-hand shift lever makes *minor* adjustments (leg muscles work slightly harder or easier with each change of gears), and the left-hand shift lever makes *major* adjustments.

The second step is learning the effect of each shift lever (there are two, remember: a large lever and a smaller one) on each side of the handlebars. Now, as you pedal slowly, concentrate on how each gear change feels to your legs as you shift continuously with just the right hand. What you'll notice is that on the right side the large lever makes pedaling easier and the small lever makes pedaling harder.

RIGHT-HAND SHIFT LEVER: Large lever = easier pedaling

Small lever = harder pedaling

• **Below-the-bar shift levers** •

Conversely, on the left side the large lever makes pedaling harder and the small lever makes pedaling easier.

LEFT-HAND SHIFT LEVER: Large lever = harder pedaling

Small lever = easier pedaling

Sure, it's a bit confusing, so don't lose patience or become disgusted with yourself when you get things mixed up at first. And know too that derailleurs (or less poetically, gear changers) aren't magic. You traced the cables from the handlebar-mounted gearshift levers to the derailleurs, remember? Well, shift—lever movement either lengthens or shortens the cable, pulling a part of the derailleur across the cogs in one direction or the other. And this "derails" the chain from one sprocket to another.

You might find it helpful to watch the chain climb onto the large sprocket up front (front-wheel sprockets are called chainwheels or chainrings; rear-wheel sprockets are called freewheel cogs) and drop to the middle and smallest chainring when you direct it to do so with your gearshift lever. Watch too as the chain runs back and

· **Over-the-bar shift levers** ·

forth across the freewheel cogs. This mental image of what actually happens when you push levers should help you keep things straight.

If you have over-the-bar shifters things are easier still, because you have only one shift lever on each side of the handlebars. Moving the right-hand shifter forward will move the chain to a larger sprocket in the rear, making it easier to pedal. Moving it back (toward the handlebar) moves the chain to a smaller sprocket in the rear, making it harder to pedal.

> **RIGHT-HAND SHIFT LEVER:** Forward = easier pedaling
>
> Backward = harder pedaling

Conversely, moving the left-hand shift lever forward makes pedaling harder, and moving it back toward the handlebar makes it easier to pedal.

> **LEFT-HAND SHIFT LEVER:** Forward = harder pedaling
>
> Backward = easier pedaling

SPROCKETS

As you have learned, the three front sprockets are called chainwheels or chainrings and are used for major gear adjustments. But for learning purposes we are going to rename these gears Granny, Ma, and Pa.

> **GRANNY:** smallest sprocket
>
> **MA:** middle sprocket
>
> **PA:** largest sprocket

In general, Granny is used when climbing tough hills or when you want to ride very slowly, such as when you're traversing extremely technical (difficult-to-cross) terrain. Ma is used over moderate ter-

• Chainrings •   **• Freewheel •**

rain or when a rider faces head winds or simply wishes to maintain a high cyclic (pedal revolutions per minute) rate. Pa is great for fast descents and those paved-road days when the weather gods have the wind at your back.

Moving to the rear wheel: Most freewheels consist of either six or seven sprockets. These, remember, in contrast to the front sprockets, are used for minor gear changes. For learning purposes we will number them one through seven, one being the largest sprocket (and closest to the spokes), and seven being the smallest sprocket (farthest from the spokes).

Gear combinations—that is, the gear you are in as a result of placing the chain on a particular front sprocket and rear sprocket combination—will be referred to in front gear/rear gear sequence. For example, we might say Pa/7, which is the largest chainring in front and the smallest sprocket in the rear.

There are two possible gear combinations that you should *not* use, however. These are Pa/1 and Granny/7 (largest front/largest rear, and smallest front/smallest rear). In each case the chain is stretched across the freewheel at a radical angle, hence the term *cross-shifting* for these combinations. The reason they should be avoided is that damage is done to the front and rear sprockets, chain, and derailleurs. But don't be extremely concerned if you

• **Granny/7 cross-shifting** •

• **Pa/1 cross-shifting** •

mistakenly force the chain into one of these gear combinations while riding; damage does not occur immediately. Learning to avoid cross-shifting, however, will greatly extend the life of your bike's transmission.

• **Pa/1 cross-shifting** •

SOFT PEDALING

It is best to "soft pedal" while shifting gears, because this reduces the strain on derailleurs. Soft pedaling refers to the slight easing up on the pedal stroke as you shift, a very easy thing to do when on a slight downhill or when traveling with fair speed on level ground. However, it is when climbing steep hills that soft pedaling during shifts is both hardest and most important to do.

One technique employed by experienced mountain bikers is to anticipate the gear needed and shift before the hardest part of the climb. If you need to shift again during the climb, or have anticipated incorrectly, try powering one stroke (pedal very hard on one downstroke) so that the momentum gained will allow soft pedaling on the next. Shift immediately after the powered stroke, because the soft pedaling during the next few seconds will ease tension on the chain, thus allowing the derailleur to move more easily.

The correct anticipation of which gear is required will come about in time, as you learn your ability in relation to hills of varying grades. Powering on the downstroke, so as to soft pedal while shifting on the next, requires practice and physical ability. Again, both will come in time.

Remember, it takes a lot of words to describe very simple shifting techniques. Jump into the saddle now (remaining in the comfortable learning environment of flat pavement for this section) and run through various gear combinations and soft pedaling; work to avoid cross-shifting. You will see how easy it is after just a little practice.

CADENCE

Most bikers work their leg muscles inefficiently by pedaling at too slow a cadence—that is, too slow a cyclic rate (pedal strokes per minute). Although you might feel stable in the saddle with a slow cadence, this will make for instability when on the trails, where you must be able to move quickly in one direction or another, around or over the obstacles you encounter.

After practicing your shifting, move on to practicing an efficient cadence, somewhere between eighty and ninety strokes per minute. Bikers talk in terms of "pushing large or small gears," a reference to the numerical gear ratio in which the larger the number, the harder it is to pedal. Pushing large gears, and the accompanying slow cadence, is not only inefficient and tough for trail riding, but also hard on the knees.

BRAKING IN A STRAIGHT LINE

A body in motion tends to stay at uniform motion in a straight line unless acted upon by an outside force.

—Isaac Newton's First Law of Motion

Learning Environment: BEGIN ON FLAT PAVEMENT, PROGRESS TO DIRT.

You might have noticed that when you apply the brakes on your mountain bike *it* stops, but you continue to move toward the handlebars. Actually, the part of you that moves forward the most is the heaviest part of you—your center of mass, or CM. In an automobile we wear seat belts to keep us from launching forward during quick stops. On a touring bike we simply push backward a bit with arms and legs. But on a mountain bike we must be more creative.

The best way to keep your CM behind the bars, where it belongs, is to learn the three-step stopping progression called "set, sit, and stop." The first of these, the set position, is assumed by keeping both legs bent equally, the crankarms (to which the pedals are attached) parallel to the ground, and your behind slightly out of the saddle.

· **"Set" position** ·

• **"Sit" position** •

You will find that this is a very strong reactive position from which you will be able to deal very well with whatever is encountered on the trail.

After trying the set position several times, move next to the sit position. Do so by first assuming the set position, then move your center of mass rearward as far as your arms will allow. As in the photo, your bottom should be off the saddle, suspended above the rear wheel, and your pedals should once again be parallel to the ground. The sit position might look and feel a bit awkward, but you'll find it a blessing when you need to brake during a descent.

Move from the set to the sit position several times, until you can assume both naturally. And now to stop. This refers to the use of your bike's brakes, though of course trees and trailside boulders will also do the trick. Both front (left-hand) and rear (right-hand—RIGHT REAR, RIGHT REAR, remember?) brakes should be applied at the same time, but with more power being applied with the right hand. When starting out you might try using just one finger on the left brake lever and a normal grip on the right.

Once you become familiar with the proper amount of braking power required, move to the handlebar/brake lever grip Ed suggests: index and next two fingers on the brake lever, the smallest

• **"Stop" position** •

finger wrapped around the handlebar. (I prefer a different grip: index finger and thumb *always* wrapped around the bar, remaining fingers on the brake lever. With this grip I find that even unexpected encounters with tree roots or sewer gratings do not yank the handlebars from my hands, and brakes can be applied instantaneously. Begin with Ed's suggested grip; your personal preference will evolve.)

Trail riding, remember, is not like touring on the open road, where hazards to your front wheel can be seen many bike lengths ahead.

• **Thumb and forefinger around bar. Ed prefers having index and next two fingers on the brake lever, and only the smallest finger around the bar.** •

On a trail or rocky road there's always the possibility of striking an unseen object and having the handlebar jerked in one direction or the other. Keeping the thumb and forefinger curled around the bar will prevent this from happening.

Practice the set, sit, and stop positions while riding in a straight line (still on pavement) until all three positions can be assumed in one fluid motion. When this begins to feel natural, increase the speed and brake harder. Greater stability can be attained by using the inside of your quads (or quadriceps, the four-part extensor muscle on the front of the thigh) to squeeze the seat as you move into the sit position. Having contact with the saddle at this point will give you more control and will be psychologically comforting.

When you have mastered this on pavement move to level gravel or dirt. Your goal should be to set, sit, and stop at a fast speed, with no skidding. If you find that you are constantly skidding the rear tire, move your CM farther over the rear wheel and/or squeeze the front brake (left hand) harder. As you get more mileage under your belt you'll learn exactly how much you need to move your CM rearward and how hard you must brake for any situation.

4 DESCENDING

Learning Environment: START OUT ON A COMFORTABLE PAVED HILL (WITH A DROP OF ONLY FIVE TO THIRTY FEET), THEN MOVE TO A DIRT HILL OF THE SAME SIZE.

To descend in a controlled manner you need only apply the same technique you've already learned for stopping in a straight line. That is, from the set position you will move your center of mass rearward, away from the handlebars. The extent to which you must move back depends on the steepness of the hill, the terrain, and your desired descent speed.

A few runs will show you that the slower your descent speed, the more you must move your CM rearward. Use both brakes when descending in a straight line on pavement, keeping two or three fingers on each lever. Remember that your left-hand (front) brake provides most of your braking power and can throw you over the handlebars in a swan dive if you fail to use the rear brake at the same time.

When you feel completely at ease riding downhill on pavement, move on to gravel or dirt. Your riding position will be the same, but braking in loose dirt or gravel is quite different. Unfortunately, the natural first reaction to any scare in the saddle is to throw on the brakes. However, a wheel that is rolling has much more traction (and thus more stability) than one that is stopped. For these slight hills, therefore, stay off your front brake during the descent and "feather" the rear brake. ("Feathering" in mountain biking means using a light touch on the brake lever, hitting it lightly many times rather than very hard once or twice.)

On long descents (which you will do later, not now) assume a comfortable sit position, squeezing the wide part of the saddle with your legs. Stand up occasionally on your pedals to reduce fatigue, but without compromising your riding position too much.

When you tackle short, steep descents or a succession of rolling hills, let the bike follow the contour of the ground while your body remains almost vertical. Vertical in relation to what? Well, to the ground if it were flat. This will automatically move your center of mass back when it needs to be back and will bring it forward when the slope levels out. If you do this correctly you will feel the bike move underneath you while your body remains almost perfectly still. The sensation will be that of stretching your arms out as the front wheel starts down the slope, and of pulling the bars back toward you as you level out.

· **Knees and elbows are slightly bent to act as shock absorbers and allow more fluid movement.** ·

· **By shifting his weight to the rear, the rider allows the unweighted front
wheel to climb easily over the rock.** ·

more times, taking your weight off the saddle as you tip the bike into the turn, but not leaning with your upper body.

This is a very strong position from which to react to an obstacle, to pull out of an unintended skid, or to move quickly into another turn. With your CM in this neutral position you have much greater control and mobility. In skiing this movement is called "angulation," for the harsh angle you are creating between the upper torso and that portion (in this case, the bike) reaching the ground.

When you've got this move down cold in the counterclockwise direction, execute it a half-dozen times riding clockwise, then make long turns in both directions on dirt or gravel. Studies show that it takes some fifty repetitions of a maneuver, performed correctly, before it is learned so well that it can be done almost without thought. So keep practicing.

SHORT TURNS AT SLOW SPEED

Set a course with rocks, paper or plastic cups, or anything that will not damage your tires if you run into them. Set these objects in a straight line, some six to eight feet apart. As your skill develops you can reduce this space.

Now ride through the course as slowly as possible, going around each object. You will find it easiest to maintain your balance by braking with the right hand only and pedaling slowly while braking. Your turns will be made primarily by turning your handlebars rather than tipping your bike. Ride through the course until you can make it without touching any of the obstacles.

When you have mastered the course with slow turns in this fashion, try riding it while keeping your rear wheel on one side of each marker and your front tire on the other. That is, whereas before both wheels went around the same side of the obstacle, now you will be twisting past them so that if the front wheel passes the rock on the rock's right side, the handlebars will be turned quickly to the left so that the rear tire passes on the rock's left side. Got it?

In this exercise you are learning to balance at very slow speed. This will be of great use when riding tricky ("technical") sections of mountain trails and also at stoplights when you do not wish to leave the pedals. Perfect your moves on pavement, then move to flat gravel or dirt.

• **Short turns at slow speed** •   • **Sharp turns at fast speed** •

SHARP TURNS AT FAST SPEED

We are now back to angulation, tipping the bike while the body remains straight up and down. To angulate in a turn you must first move into the set position, because with your body out of the saddle it is very easy to tip the bike to either side. In this maneuver you will not be turning the handlebars as much to turn the bike, but will be tipping the bike around the obstacles instead. The photo shows Ed's center of mass almost perfectly straight (perpendicular to the ground) while the bike leans over at a great angle.

This method of turning enables you to make short, quick turns at high speeds. Try this technique now, beginning on pavement at only moderate speed and riding through the same course you set up for the short turns at slow speed. As it becomes easier for you to accomplish, pick up speed.

5

TURNING

Each of the three turns you will learn in this chapter—long turn at medium speed, short turn at slow speed, and sharp turn at fast speed—should first be practiced on

pavement, then on dirt or gravel. We will begin with the easiest, the long turn.

LONG TURN AT MEDIUM SPEED

In a large, preferably empty parking lot, use a large rock or something else easily visible to designate a turnaround point some thirty-five or forty paces from where you will begin riding. Now, at medium speed, ride around that marker and back to your starting point, in a counterclockwise direction.

Do it a second time, but brake with the right hand only; all fingers of the left hand should be wrapped around the handlebar only. This is important, because when you progress to a looser surface, tighter turns, and greater speed, the use of that front (left-hand) brake can cause the bike to slide right out from under you.

Next, make another long turn, and while you are braking with the right hand only put all your weight on the outside (right) pedal. This will push the outside pedal to the bottom of the stroke (six o'clock position, see photo above), ensuring that the inside (left) pedal is up (twelve o'clock position).

Why is this important? Jump out of the saddle, place the left pedal at the bottom of the stroke, then walk around to the front of the bike and take hold of both handlebars. Now lean the bike to the right, the same direction in which the bike is leaning when you make a counterclockwise turn. Notice that you do not have to lean the bike very far at all before the left pedal touches the ground. If this were to happen while you were riding, there is a good chance that you would be thrown.

Okay, make another long turn around your marker, still at medium speed, still counterclockwise, still braking with your right hand only and pushing down on the outside (right) pedal so as to bring the left pedal high and away from the ground. But this time try pointing your inside (left) knee toward the inside of the turn. This maneuver, in addition to the other techniques, will help you "commit to the turn" in a nice, stable arc.

Practice these three elements (right-hand braking, outside foot pressure, inside knee direction) five or six more times. When you can execute all three simultaneously, without effort, begin lifting yourself slightly out of the saddle as the bike tips under you. Try this several

6
RIDING OVER OBSTACLES

Learning Environment: FLAT PAVEMENT, SHALLOW GRAVEL, OR GOOD (NOT VERY LOOSE) DIRT; YOU WILL NEED THREE STICKS OR BOARDS WITH DIAMETERS OF APPROXIMATELY ONE, THREE, AND SIX INCHES.

No matter where you pedal you will encounter some kind of obstacle in your path. Whether this is a rock, stick, log, or curb, you will have to decide on a plan of

• **Rolling over obstacle from Set/Sit positions** •

attack: riding around it, riding right over it, hopping it, or carrying your bike across it. You have already learned how to turn around an obstacle. In this chapter you will learn how to roll over and hop it.

ROLLING OVER AN OBSTACLE

Two things are necessary for your front wheel to roll successfully over an object in your path: (1) the front wheel must be made "light," and (2) the front wheel must be turning freely (no braking). You will make your front wheel light by moving into the set and sit positions. This will move your center of mass backward, thus taking weight off the front wheel. To ensure that the front wheel is turning freely as you go over the obstacle, keep the fingers of both hands wrapped around the handlebar, not the brake lever. (You can, of course, brake before or after the obstacle, but the front wheel *must* be revolving when it encounters the stick.) Make a few runs over the smallest (one-inch diameter) stick or board.

When obstacles reach the size of approximately three inches in diameter, you must become a bit more aggressive in getting the front wheel off the ground. Move into the set and sit positions as

• **Lifting front tire over obstacle** •

• Lifting rear tire over obstacle •

• Hopping over an obstacle •

before, keep your hands off the brakes, and lift the front wheel (by pulling up on the handlebars) just as the front tire encounters the obstacle. As you practice this you will find that the first contact with the stick will already bump your front tire into the air somewhat; by lifting the handlebars you are simply accentuating the wheel's natural movement. This technique will work for ninety percent of the obstacles you'll encounter during trail riding.

Now, imagine meeting up with a fairly smooth, round tree limb some three inches in diameter and long enough to stretch across a loose-surface trail. Rolling over this object will cause it to move when your rear tire strikes it. You reduce the forward pressure exerted against the obstacle by the front wheel by pulling up on the handlebars, but your rear tire has no such assistance.

There are two techniques that will help that rear tire over the obstacle. First, you can begin pedaling as soon as your front tire is over the object; the torque applied to the rear wheel will assist it in climbing up and over. Second, use center-of-mass movement to lighten the rear wheel. Just as you lightened the front wheel by moving into the sit position, now you will move your CM forward (toward the handlebars) as soon as your front wheel clears the object.

Both these maneuvers are easily employed on level or near-level terrain. However, you must be extremely careful when you encounter a loose object during a steep descent while trail riding. Moving your center of mass forward a lot during a steep descent can lighten the rear wheel too much, causing a headplant (a dive over the handlebars, usually accompanied by the bike flipping up and over you). Don't try a steep descent now, of course, but when you do, go easy on the degree to which you move your CM forward. All that is required is enough movement to reduce the weight on that rear wheel, and wheel-weight reduction depends on the grade (the steepness of a hill). By keeping this thought in mind and experimenting on hills of differing grades, you will soon know intuitively how far you must move your center of mass forward to clear a loose object on the trail.

HOPPING OVER AN OBSTACLE

When you are riding fast and suddenly face an obstacle it is best, if possible, to clear it entirely by hopping over it. At high speed even minor contact can throw you off balance.

Practice this technique on smooth, level ground. Riding at moderate speed (to start out), approach the obstacle, stop pedaling just before you reach it, coil your body over the top tube (the tube running parallel to the ground, from the saddle to the handlebars), then push your center of mass straight up. If you do this correctly the bike should remain parallel to the ground as it floats into the air.

You will probably find during your first few attempts that the rear wheel remains stuck to the ground. This could be because you are approaching the obstacle at too slow a speed. If this remains a problem even when you increase speed, use your arms as levers to pry yourself from the earth. That is, while keeping your wrists straight and hands tight around the bars, quickly rotate your elbows forward at the moment you attempt the hop. (Practice this a few times before riding; the initial movement resembles a flap of wings in reverse.)

Begin by hopping over shadows, cracks in the dirt or pavement, or very small sticks. Move up to larger obstacles, experimenting with the different speeds required to clear things of increasing size.

7
CLIMBING

Even the most powerful riders will "lose" a hill if they fail to learn the three essential techniques: pedaling in circles, maintaining traction, and starting on a hill. As you practice each of these maneuvers remember not to allow your

strength alone to power you to the top; choose a tougher or longer grade if necessary, but concentrate on *technique*. No matter how strong the rider, there is a hill out there that can only be "won" by combining strength and finesse.

PEDALING IN CIRCLES

All riders know that pedals travel in a circle. So there's no choice but to pedal around the clock, right? Well, there is a critical difference between allowing your pedals to follow their natural arc and pedaling strongly and efficiently by making use of every part of that revolution.

Beginning riders work their pedals like pistons, up and down, up and down. But this provides power during only fifty percent of each pedal stroke—the downward movement of that pedal arc. Practice the following instead. As the pedal begins its descent (from the twelve o'clock position to one o'clock and on to six), push forward and down with full power. Then, as the pedal reaches its lowest point (six o'clock), do not simply allow the dead weight of that pedal, foot, and leg to be pushed backward and up by the down-

• **Toeclip and strap** •

ward thrust of the opposite pedal. Instead, pull back and up (toward twelve o'clock again) on that pedal. Remember, you do possess muscles in each leg that pull up as well as push down.

Practice this technique on the hill you've chosen for this section, but keep in mind that pedaling on the level is also vastly improved when power is applied throughout every stroke of each pedal. Be advised that the effectiveness of this technique is far less for those riders who do not use toeclips and straps. For this reason, plus the benefit they provide of keeping feet securely on the pedals, you will find that most trail riders use the clips-and-straps combination. Very few riders, however, cinch the straps tightly when pedaling trails or commuting.

MAINTAINING TRACTION

Once you have perfected your pedal stroke you will have done much to reduce spinning out on loose surfaces because of the *constant* power being applied to that rear wheel. However, even greater traction can be attained by adding weight to the rear wheel. This is done by pulling up on the handlebars while staying in the saddle and lowering your chest toward the bars at the same time. In this fashion sufficient CM weight is placed over the rear tire, but enough is kept forward to keep the front tire on the ground.

STARTING ON A HILL

Starting on a hill is one of the most difficult things to accomplish in mountain biking. The key to success lies in that first pedal stroke, so if you have the space point your bike so that you are at a slight angle across the hill. With your downhill pedal at about two o'clock, squeeze both brakes to hold yourself in position. Now release your brakes and make that first pedal stroke as if you are on solid, treacherous ice. Why? Because in order to make that rear wheel grip the dirt you must pedal softly and slowly. (You begin with your downhill pedal because the uphill pedal could more easily hit the dirt on a steep hill.)

After that first stroke, when you have found the opposite pedal with your other foot, you will have to begin pedaling faster and harder in order to power up the hill. Attempting to enter toeclips with that second foot at such a time is very difficult, so don't concern yourself about it until a break in the grade allows the opportunity.

PUSHING OR PORTAGING

With the techniques you have just learned, and a modicum of strength, you should be able to stay in the saddle for the great majority of hills you'll encounter. You can still reach the top of those grades that prove too steep, of course, by pushing or portaging your bike.

Pushing on very steep hills is usually accomplished with a hand on either end of the handlebars and the rider leaning forward over the front wheel. When this grows tiresome, however, try keeping the left hand on the handlebar end nearer you and the right hand curled around the back of the saddle (heel of the hand on the saddle top, knuckles pointed to the rear tire, fingers cupped under). This position is especially good for lifting the rear end over obstacles.

· **Portaging a bike** ·

• **Preparing to portage** •

Portaging a bike is a bit more involved. First, as you see being done in the photo, push the left pedal into the nine o'clock position. Second, after using the right hand to hoist the bike by its top tube, reach through the main-frame triangle and grab hold of the handlebars, while the left hand reaches up to the saddle.

In this manner the pedal will be tucked to the side of the hip, the crankarm will rest comfortably against the small of the back, and the top tube will lie across the shoulders. In this position you can carry the bike easily for a great distance, as well as maneuver the bike's front and rear wheels around obstacles (through the control provided by your grip on both the saddle and the handlebars).

Very short portages can be handled in the manner that most of us carry bikes down a flight of stairs, by simply placing the pedal nearest you at nine o'clock, cupping a hand beneath the top tube (tube running from saddle to handlebars) close to the saddle, then lifting the bike to the shoulder. Brace the top part of the arm used to lift the bike against the seat tube (tube running from saddle to pedals), and take off.

· Lifting the bike ·

· A short portage ·

8

TRAIL ETIQUETTE

Knowing how to pedal the trails is not the same as understanding how to conduct oneself while doing so. That is, although even most first-time mountain bikers know it is unlawful to ride in designated wilderness areas or to pedal trails "signed" against bike travel, not everyone is sensitive to the

• **Good descent technique. While the lack of a helmet endangers only this rider's head, his disregard of the off-limits sign endangers all mountain bikers' riding privileges—on this trail and everywhere.** •

damage that results when wet terrain is rutted by mountain bike tires or knows what to do when encountering hikers, horses, or other trail users.

In an attempt to defuse the conflict between cyclists and hikers or equestrians (and thereby deter further trail closings to mountain bikes), many off-road bicycle organizations have devised guidelines for safe, responsible trail use. One of the largest of these—NORBA (National Off-Road Bicycle Association)—offers the following code of behavior:

1. I will yield the right of way to other nonmotorized recreationists. I realize that people judge all cyclists by my actions.

2. I will slow down and use caution when approaching or overtaking another and will make my presence known well in advance.

3. I will maintain control of my speed at all times and will approach turns in anticipation of someone around the bend.

• **Dennis Coello winter touring in Colorado.** •

4. I will stay on designated trails to avoid trampling native vegetation and minimize potential erosion to trails by not using muddy trails or short-cutting switchbacks.

5. I will not disturb wildlife or livestock.

6. I will not litter. I will pack out what I pack in, and pack out more than my share whenever possible.

7. I will respect public and private property, including trail use signs and no trespassing signs, and I will leave gates as I have found them.

8. I will always be self-sufficient, and my destination and travel speed will be determined by my ability, my equipment, the terrain, and the present and potential weather conditions.

9. I will not travel solo when bikepacking in remote areas. I will leave word of my destination and when I plan to return.

10. I will observe the practice of minimum-impact bicycling by "taking only pictures and memories and leaving only waffle prints."

11. I will always wear a helmet when I ride.

NORBA's code is surely the best known, but in my estimation a far superior code of ethics for mountain bikers is distributed by Utah's Wasatch-Cache National Forest office. It thankfully avoids NORBA's overly protective sentiments about never riding solo in remote areas. Many of us, after all, use mountain bikes as jeeps to reach the backcountry. Sometimes we prefer to be absolutely alone and haven't a clue when we'll return. Responsible backcountry travel includes taking care of both the environment *and* of oneself.

STUDY A FOREST MAP BEFORE YOU RIDE Currently, bicycles are permitted on roads and designated trails within the Wasatch-Cache National Forest except in designated wilderness areas. If your route crosses private land, it is your responsibility to obtain right of way permission from the land owner.

KEEP GROUPS SMALL Riding in large groups degrades the outdoor experience for others, can disturb wildlife, and usually leads to greater resource damage.

AVOID RIDING ON WET TRAILS Bicycle tires leave ruts in wet trails. These ruts concentrate runoff and accelerate erosion. Postponing a ride when the trails are wet will preserve the trails for future use.

· Mountain bikes can bring us to remote, beautiful places . . . ·

STAY ON ROADS AND TRAILS Riding cross-country destroys vegetation and damages the soil.

———

ALWAYS YIELD TO OTHERS Trails are shared by hikers, horses, and bicycles. Move off the trail to allow horses to pass and stop to allow hikers adequate room to share the trail. Simply yelling "bicycle" is not acceptable.

———

CONTROL YOUR SPEED Excessive speed endangers yourself and other forest users.

———

AVOID WHEEL LOCK-UP AND SPIN-OUT Steep terrain is especially vulnerable to trail wear. Locking brakes on steep descents, or when stopping, needlessly damages trails. If a slope is steep enough to require locking wheels and skidding, dismount and walk your bicycle. Likewise, if an ascent is so steep your rear wheel slips and spins, dismount and walk your bicycle.

———

PROTECT WATERBARS AND SWITCHBACKS Waterbars, the rock and log drains built to direct water off trails, protect trails from erosion. When you encounter a waterbar, ride directly over the top or dismount and walk your bicycle. Riding around the ends of waterbars destroys them and speeds erosion. Skidding around switchback corners shortens trail life. Slow for switchback corners and keep your wheels rolling.

———

IF YOU ABUSE IT—YOU LOSE IT Mountain bikes are relative newcomers to the forest and must prove themselves responsible trail users. By following the guidelines above, and by participating in trail maintenance service projects, bicyclists can help avoid closures which would prevent them from using trails.

———

• . . . but at what price to the environment? •

9
URBAN JUNGLES

Ask one of America's two million bike commuters why they pedal to work and school and you'll hear a host of answers: It's economical, it's good exercise, it's environmentally sound, it puts them more in tune with the natural world.

• **The suit looks good, but the hat's too soft to help in case of an accident. Notice fenders and this commuter's use of pants clips.** •

Ask one of America's two million bike commuters what kind of bike is best for urban travel and you'll probably hear only three short words: a mountain bike.

Why? Well, think first about the riding techniques you've already learned in this book. Next, imagine yourself downtown in traffic during rush hour, with a Buick suddenly cutting you off and forcing you into the curb. A moment of sheer terror? Nah, not on an ATB. With a quick center-of-mass movement and pull of the handlebars the curb can be hopped as easily as any practice log on the trail.

Mountain bikes are infinitely safer commuting machines than their spindly, unstable, skinny-tired cousins, prone as they are to over-reacting when they hit a pothole or a piece of glass. Add to this mechanical advantage the skills developed through trail riding and you have a late-twentieth-century creation designed to help you survive today's paved jungles. Just imagine yourself jumping curbs, twisting past sewer gratings, stopping suddenly for red lights or car doors opening in your face, rolling over obstacles (no, not pedestrians) without losing your balance. Yes, all the savvy of an animal in the bush is necessary to negotiate a business district today without winding up as a hood ornament. But by this point in the book you've already come a long way.

A few add-on items will make your city travel safer and more enjoyable. A rearview mirror, attached to your helmet or left handlebar, is a must. Very wide fenders will shield your front and back from road spray; the newest models snap into place in minutes. A survey of mountain bike tires would require a complete chapter, but there are many models of "Slicks" and "Streetsters" that are almost as thin as touring tires, Kevlar belted to guard against flats, and into which you can pack a hundred psi (pounds per square inch of air pressure) for fast, *fast* commutes.

Add a rack (in the rear at least) to get books and briefcase off your back; a set of good panniers with rain covers; a rear reflector, pedal reflectors, and light for those dark early morning/late afternoon winter commutes; and a long-shackle U-lock that will wrap around both your front wheel and down tube (tube running from handlebars to pedals). And though the use of brand names is usually avoided when suggesting gear, check out a Belt Beacon. This lightweight, inexpensive clip-on light flashes amber to all onlookers. Wear it and you're likely to be hit only by moths.

This is a book about riding techniques, not equipment or bike design, but a word on gearing is necessary here. Just as trail riders

• One of America's 4 million bike commuters. •

soon learn that a 24-tooth smallest chainring is mandatory for taking the toughest grades, commuters often find that they are in need of a higher (harder) gear when pedaling pavement. Why? Mountain bikes are geared lower than thin-tire touring bikes. ATBs must be easier to pedal because of their larger, lower-pressure tires, upright handlebars, and the far slower off-road terrain. But when commuters change tires and hit the pavement, they are soon outpedaling their highest gears.

Many mountain bikes today still come with chainrings of 28/38/48 (28 teeth, 38 teeth, etc.) and freewheels running from a small of 14 (teeth) to a large of only 30. Hard-core hill climbers drop the 28-tooth chainring to a 24 and increase the size of the largest freewheel cog to 32 or even 34 (thus lowering the lowest gear considerably). Moving in the opposite direction, impatient commuters switch the 48-tooth chainring to a 52 and drop the smallest freewheel cog to 13 or even 12 teeth.

Talk to your bike shop salespeople if you're mystified by the numbers. Don't worry, they'll take the time to explain things in detail, will probably give you their personal views on gearing, and won't even be upset if you leave without dropping a dime. We aren't, after all, talking about buying a car.

10

BACKCOUNTRY TOURING

Only one element of back-country touring makes that riding experience greatly different from the one enjoyed on local day tours: weight. Most trail riders carry an absolute minimum of gear, stuffed into a tiny under-the-saddle seat bag or fanny pack. But head into the hills or woods or desert for a few days and everything changes. Racks, packs, tent, sleeping bag, cooking gear, clothes—the list of required equipment goes on and on. Hard-core trail riders talk in terms of grams when choosing components and ounces when packing their gear. But tourers talk in pounds.

And it is those pounds that you must learn to pedal. You already know the techniques necessary for getting you and your bike any-where. But now you'll find that center-of-mass movements, and the application of force to pedals and handlebars, must all be accentu-ated. Begin adding weight to the bike gradually, weeks before the intended tour. And start building the required lower- *and* upper-torso strength long before that.

LOADING TIPS

Loading distribution on a thin-tire bike is simple:

1. Weight should be relatively even on both sides.

* In this chapter I borrow heavily from the far more thorough treatment of all aspects of mountain bikes in my book *The Complete Mountain Biker* (New York: Lyons & Burford, 1989).

2. Weight should be distributed between the front and rear of the bike in roughly a one-third/two-thirds proportion.

3. Whenever possible, weight should be carried low and close to the frame.

Loading a mountain bike the same way works well on good dirt roads and even on all but the worst of chewed-up jeep roads and double-tracks (these are the dual tracks made by a jeep or other vehicle, with grass, weeds, or rocks between). But jump on a single-track (literally a single track through grass or brush or over rocky terrain, often created by deer, elk, or backpackers) and you'll probably find it necessary to lessen your load up front. Lifting that front wheel is tough when hauling heavy front panniers. (*Note:* Although low-riding panniers are fine for pavement tours, they should be avoided when off-road. Drop into a rut only a few inches deep with low-riders and you'll wind up in camp without all your packs.)

Long before the ride you should give thought to the effect of loaded touring on bodily comfort. The saddle that works great for day rides may cause you to curse it after a few hours of loaded touring. Heavy loads force your rear end deeper into the saddle; a bit of padding will be appreciated. However, any saddle will make you sore if you haven't broken it in; your rump needs time to break in as well.

And while we're on the subject of preparing your body for a tour, even unloaded trail riding demands what exercise physiologists call the "triad of physical fitness"—strength, endurance, and flexibility. Loaded touring requires all these in spades.

READING TOPOGRAPHIC MAPS

Motorists do quite well with "flat" maps—those that indicate only the distance between two points—because all that's required to handle steep grades is greater pressure on the gas pedal. Mountain bikers, however, must have a good idea of the upcoming gain or loss of elevation to compute (in even the most general terms) how many hours or days a route will take. Other riders or guidebooks can supply this information. But another sure source (and far more

reliable, many times, than other riders) is topographic maps—*topos* for short.

Topos indicate elevation through the use of "contour lines." The theory is simple, and in half an hour a neophyte can be reading topos like a pro. At the bottom of each map is a "contour interval" designation of so many feet. Large-scale, single-state maps (1:500,000 scale; one inch equals eight linear miles) have an interval of five hundred feet. That is, every time a contour line is encountered along your route you will be gaining or losing five hundred feet of elevation (occasional figures on these lines tell you whether that's up- or downhill). If your path is free of these lines you're pedaling the plains, or perhaps struggling up and zooming down a lot of 499-foot hills that don't show up. If half a dozen of these contour lines exist in close proximity, you know you're pulling a mountain pass.

The next scale of topos I sometimes use to get an overall feel for a region I'm touring is 1:250,000; one inch equals four miles, contour interval of two hundred feet. These are obviously far more detailed, but still insufficient for the exacting needs of mountain bikers. After all, a series of steep one-hundred-foot climbs can have you panting in an hour; a day of them will see you too tired to set up your tent, or , heaven forbid, your motel reservation given to a motorist.

Better by far for those on fat tires is the 1:62,500 scale; one inch equals one mile, contour interval of eighty feet. But best of all is the 1:24,000 scale (known as 7.5 minute, pronounced "seven-and-a-half-minute"); one inch equals two thousand linear feet, contour interval most often of forty feet. The detail on these last maps is amazing, and with the addition of a planimeter (accent on the second syllable) you will have an excellent idea of what lies ahead. (Sometimes called simply a map measurer, a planimeter has a tiny metal wheel that you roll along the map; a needle and gauge compute the inches traveled, and you multiply this by whatever scale map you're using. This gives you your distance; the contour lines provide the elevation gain and loss.)

Topographic maps also provide detailed road classifications. Different colorings or markings indicate the categories of interstate, heavy-duty, medium-duty, light-duty, unimproved dirt roads, and jeep trails. Map symbols include everything from footbridges and overpasses to dams and canals. Various shadings indicate swamps, wooded marshes, vineyards, orchards, and more. If your route takes you past a glacier, your topo will show you the best way around it.

But this detail comes at a cost—that of so many maps being required for relatively short rides. For example, thirteen 7.5-minute maps are necessary to cover the distance of the tough, unpaved, historic 107-mile Lolo Trail (Lewis and Clark's, and the Nez Perce's, trail across the Bitterroot Mountains). Not wishing to ruin my topos by cramming them into bike bags or exposing them to rain (or, at mountaintops, the rain of perspiration), I photocopy them and leave the originals at home.

Some copy centers have machines large enough to handle an entire 7.5-minute map, but I prefer to use a regular (less expensive) machine, set on 11-by-17-inch size, and copy only that portion of the map covering my trail. To avoid confusion I number these copies sequentially. Before the trip I use a colorful "hi-liter" to highlight my intended route but not obscure it. When on the trail I sometimes note locations of certain sites (especially when following historic routes) on my copies. But if not they serve perfectly for starting campfires.

If there's a bike shop in an area well known for its bike trails, chances are the shop will carry the topos you'll need. But don't bank on it. Major university libraries and some public libraries carry them, as do other specialty outdoor stores. But if you can't find them locally you can mail order the maps from one of two USGS (United States Geological Survey) offices.

For areas west of the Mississippi River:

USGS-ESIC
Box 25046
Federal Center
MS 504
Denver, CO 80225-0046

For areas east of the Mississippi River:

USGS-ESIC
Reston
507 National Center
Reston, VA 22092

Write first for an index, a price list, and a free copy of the booklet *Topographic Maps*. This will take all the mystery out of contour lines and symbols.

A second excellent series of maps available to mountain bikers is that put out by the United States Forest Service. If your trail runs through an area designated as a national forest, look in the phone book (White Pages) under the United States government listings, find the Department of Agriculture heading, and then run your finger through that section until you find the Forest Service. Give them a call and they'll provide the address of the regional Forest Service office, from which you can obtain the appropriate map.

WATER IN THE BACKCOUNTRY

It is almost axiomatic that mountain bike tourers will *underesti-*mate the quantity of water they'll need. This is understandable, given that water weighs in at a whopping eight pounds per gallon. It is only natural that at home, near taps with a seemingly endless

supply of the stuff, we can convince ourselves that we need less water—and therefore less weight.

But there is one simple physiological fact that should be recalled by every rider: A human working hard in ninety-degree temperature needs approximately ten quarts of fluids every day. Ten quarts. That's two and a half gallons. That's *twelve* large water bottles, or *sixteen* small ones, for a total water weight of twenty pounds.

Two things should be obvious from these facts. One, you should pack along two or three large bottles even for short multihour rides. And two, because you will be unable to carry all the water you'll need for several days, you must be able to find and purify water along the way.

Locating water sources can be done by talking to other riders, by consulting topos, and by knowing the effect of the seasons on the land you'll be traveling. Purifying the water you are fortunate enough to locate can be done in several ways. Boiling for ten minutes (plus one additional minute for each one thousand feet of elevation above sea level) will kill all bacteria and viruses. But that

• **Hole-in-the-Rock Trail, Utah. That's right, seven water bottles—two large and five small for a total of 156 ounces, or almost five quarts. In weight that equals ten pounds, and yet it is only *half* the water you'll need if riding hard for a day in ninety-degree heat. The moral: you cannot possibly carry enough; know where to find water, and how to purify it.** •

probably isn't how you planned to spend your bike tour. Besides, who wants to pack a stove on every trip, or all the fuel necessary for this amount of boiling, or denude the countryside for wood?

Luckily, there is a better way. Many riders pack along effective, inexpensive, and only slightly distasteful tetraglycine hydroperiodide tablets (sold under the names of Potable Aqua, Globaline, Coughlan's, and others). Some invest in portable, lightweight purifiers that filter out the crud. All three purification methods are a bother, but because of the unfortunate prevalence of *Giardia* you *must* use one of them to be sure.

And just to convince you to take care, a brief word on this infamous bug. *Giardia*, short for *Giardia lamblia*, was known as the "backpacker's bane" until we mountain bikers expropriated it. It is a waterborne parasite that begins its life cycle when swallowed, and one to four weeks later has its host (you) bloated, vomiting, shivering with chills, and living in the bathroom. And don't think the water's pure just because you can't *see* any bugs doing laps in your water bottle. The parasite is invisible to the naked eye, but you'll sure know it's around once you've swallowed it.

FOOD IN THE BACKCOUNTRY

Many thin-tire tourers, anxious to save on weight and usually not more than a couple of hours from a store or cafe, decide against packing a stove. I do quite well on most paved tours with my always-in-the-pannier complement of peanut butter, bread, jam, and cheese, supplemented daily by store purchases of fresh fruit and candy bars and trips to local cafes.

But things are different in the backcountry, especially when you're planning to be away from towns for days on end. In warmer seasons and in terrain that I anticipate will offer fuel I still forgo a stove, simply to save the weight. But in early spring, late fall, and especially in winter I add the ounces to my load. When the wood is wet, or I'm too tired (read lazy) to build a fire, nothing beats producing BTUs with the flick of a match.

What does one cook? I start the evening meal, and end it, with instant coffee. In between I boil a couple of cups of water, throw in two handfuls of enriched precooked instant rice, sprinkle half a box of instant soup and some jerky into the concoction, and roughly five minutes later I'm chowing down.

Breakfast is usually granola, over which I pour powdered milk, then add water and stir. The stove is cranked up only for coffee, or hot oats (liberally impregnated with raisins) if the temperature is in the teens and the skies are promising snow.

This leaves only lunch, and the twenty or so snack breaks between sunup and when I blow my candle lantern out and go to bed.

Midday meals are always uncooked, unless it's been a wet and sloppy ride and I suddenly spy a dry, inviting rock overhang. But usually it's peanut butter, jam, bread, and cheese, or sage rubbed between the hands and sprinkled over the peanut butter when the jam is gone. Snacks are anything I happened to have a fancy for the last day before the ride and threw into the bike bags. But almost always I pack quantities of dried fruit and jerky.

Here are a few good food tips:

1. Pack your peanut butter and jam, and *especially* any honey, in high-quality plastic screw-lid jars. I've yet to meet a snap-lock lid that can handle a bike ride.

2. You'll save yourself a lot of money in the long run if you, and perhaps some of your biking or hiking friends, invest in a dehydrator. They're great for deer, elk, and beef jerky and will expand your menu of dried fruits far beyond that offered by even the best-stocked health-food stores.

3. Do *not* keep food, or bags or clothing impregnated with the smell of food, in your tent overnight when you're in bear country. Pack a shank of parachute cord or lightweight rope and suspend these items in a sack at least ten feet off the ground.

RAIN, SNOW, AND COLD

When fighting rain or snow or the fear of ice when it gets cold, commuters and tourers must rely on a riding technique covered early in this book: the ability to go slow. Under all adverse weather conditions it is usually more difficult to see far ahead and thus to react in time to obstacles in your path. In addition, there is the mechanical disadvantage of wet brake pads attempting to stop a slick, spinning metal wheel rim. Wide, knobby tires do wonders in helping you to stay upright in rain and flakes, but fast riding offsets this advantage and will soon have you learning to fall. In short, pedal evenly, pedal slowly, and by all means, if it's practical, pedal before dark.

When it comes to clothing, mountain bikers have two major choices if they wish to remain dry in rain and snow—the poncho/chaps combination or a rainsuit. I use a rainsuit for midwinter commutes and tours, a poncho and chaps for all other seasons. The rainsuit has a problem with heat buildup. No matter the material,

• Even a large garbage bag helps in a pinch, but it does little to protect your lower torso. •

pedal inside a suit and after a while you'll feel as if you're working out in a greenhouse. This makes them great when it's raining and the temperature is near or below the freezing point, but horrible when it's warm.

Bike ponchos, on the other hand, are designed to allow air to circulate around the body while still shedding rain. This works because of their unique design—a tentlike, waterproof pullover, with a back flap tying about the waist and thumb loops in the front to stretch this portion out to the handlebars. It is especially critical when commuting, or touring through the occasional town, to have a poncho hood that can be drawn tightly around the face. If this isn't done you will lose your peripheral vision, thereby greatly decreasing your chances of avoiding accidents.

Ponchos work on the top, but a hard or horizontal rain (when it comes in sheets blown by ferocious winds) can still soak your lower torso. And this is where the chaps come in. Rain pants can be worn, but these close off the crotch and waist to airflow, causing dampness inside. Chaps, however, are simple waterproof tubes that tie at the waist to a belt loop, thereby allowing air to circulate. The chaps

· Utah's Red Canyon near Bryce National Park ·

bottoms overlap the gaiters (these shoe coverings are discussed next), which in turn overlap the open portions of shoes or boots. It is a system similar to roof tiles, with successive, rain-shedding layers.

(*Note:* Don't think you have to buy a new poncho/chaps outfit if yours begins to leak. The K-Kote waterproofing can be restored with products such as Re-Kote and Flex-Dri, available in some outdoor shops and catalogues.)

Designed to shed water away from the tops of boots or shoes, gaiters attach beneath the instep (with a strap) and to the laces (with a hook) and are usually zippered up the back or side, though front zippers (with a covering flap) are my preference. I also prefer very long gaiters that reach just below the knee, because on most days these will shed almost all the rain that blows beneath your poncho as well as protect you from road splash. (When the rain isn't hard I ride with poncho and gaiters only, leaving the chaps for wetter days.) Choose the more expensive, breathable fabrics for your gaiters and you won't get perspiration buildup at the ankles.

I like lightweight ankle-length boots for foul-weather riding and waterproof them with Snow Seal or saddle soap. Madden (a Boulder, Colorado, pannier company) makes an excellent pair of rain boots designed to fit over riding shoes, with heavy packcloth uppers and a very tough cordura sole. These aren't the only brand made, but they should serve as a point of comparison.

I use goggles to keep the rain from my glasses, a wide headband or silk hat beneath my helmet for warmth, and a neoprene face mask when it's bitter cold. In fact, on the coldest winter tours I also spread a very thin coating of vaseline on my face to prevent frostbite. So you thought this happened only in Jack London stories? Think again: Mountain bikers greatly increase this hazard by their speed of travel.

This increased hazard is called "wind chill," a reference to the wind's cooling effect on exposed flesh. For example, if the temperature is 10 degrees F and the wind is blowing at 20 miles per hour (or if the wind isn't blowing at all, but you are riding at that speed), the wind-chill effect (that is, the actual temperature to which your skin reacts) is *minus* 32 degrees. If you are riding in wet conditions things are even worse—the wind chill effect would then be minus 74 degrees!

When it comes to your torso, follow the principle of layering. A heavy coat might feel good when you start riding on a cold morning, but after a while you'll sweat up and be faced with the uncomfortable choices of removing it and freezing or bearing with the heat and bulk. Try instead layers of clothes that can be easily and quickly put on or off, as the weather and physical difficulty of the ride demands. In winter I begin with two-piece capilene long underwear, then a shirt and canvas riding pants, then a sweater and windproof outer shell and/or a vest for further insulation. Always remember to pack enough to keep you warm when you're out of the saddle as well. It's a whole lot colder when you aren't pedaling.

FIRST AID

Chances are that the most damage you'll ever do yourself when mountain biking is a tree branch scrape or sunburn. But just in case I pack the following in double zip-lock bags and *never* hit the trail without making sure the kit is in my pannier.

- Sunscreen
- Aspirin
- Butterfly closure bandages (think of these as Band-Aid stitches)
- Band-Aids
- Gauze compress pads (a half-dozen 4-by-4 inch)
- Gauze (one roll)
- Ace bandages or Spenco joint wraps

- Benadryl (an antihistamine to guard against allergic reactions)
- Water-purification tablets
- Moleskin/Spenco Second Skin
- Antiseptic (e.g., hydrogen peroxide, iodine, Mercurochrome)
- Snakebite kit (read the directions *before* you're bitten)

It should be obvious that you will have to repack some of these items for the road. I prefer using watertight plastic 35mm film cannisters (of which I have an abundance; if you don't spend a lot of time behind a lens I suggest you call a large film processing lab, as they often have empty cannisters they will give away or sell for a nominal fee), which I label by writing the contents on paper, cutting out the tiny block, then taping it in place.

One last point. For cactus-country tours and even weekend desert rides, I remove my snakebite kit from the double zip-lock bags and keep it closer to me. It is, after all, one item you will want to reach in a hurry.

11

ON-THE-TRAIL REPAIRS

Few mountain bikers agree on which tools are absolutely essential. The following list was offered by the two bike shop mechanics (and excellent trail riders), Ken Gron-

seth and Brad Hansen, who helped me write *The Mountain Bike Repair Book*:

- Tire levers
- Spare tube and patch kit
- Air pump
- Allen wrenches: 3, 4, 5, and 6 mm

- Six-inch crescent: adjustable-end wrench
- Small screwdriver: flat-blade tip
- Chain rivet tool
- Spoke wrench

That was what they suggested as the absolute minimum. But when I asked them what else *they* carried on the trail, the following were added:

- Channel locks—with handles sawn off to approximately six inches (you can also buy them that size)
- Air gauge—pencil-type; when pushing tires to lowest possible pressures it is important to be accurate
- Tube valve cap—metal kind, with valve-stem remover
- Baling wire—a ten-inch length; good for temporary repair if something big breaks
- Duct tape—small five-foot roll;

good for temporary repair if something small breaks, and can also be used as tire boot if nothing better is present

- Boot material—a small piece of old sew-up tire works best; large tube patch is a good substitute
- Spare chain link
- Rear derailleur pulley
- Spare nuts and bolts
- Paper towel and tube of water-less hand cleaner

For my own longer, heavily laden backcountry tours I add to the list extra spokes, freewheel tool, cone wrenches, cotterless crank removal tolls, and a pocket vise (or chain whip or Cassette Cracker; whichever tool your particular bike requires to replace broken spokes on the freewheel side). But I'm the only person I know who has ever had trouble with spokes breaking on a mountain bike. I attribute that solely to one poorly laced wheel I had on tour years ago (I've never broken one since) and to the fact that I almost never ride without an accompanying waist pack with at least twenty-five pounds of photographic gear, and panniers filled as well. In short, hit the trails with the tools listed above and you'll be in fine shape, as long as you start out with a bike in good working order.

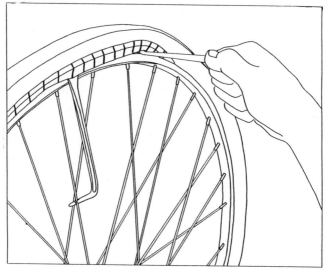

· **Tire levers at work** ·

FLATS

The far heavier rubber on mountain bike tires means far fewer flats for them than their thin-tire cousins. Nevertheless, even if you choose Kevlar belts or tire liners (thin plastic sheaths that line the inside of the tire, protecting the tube from penetrations) you will undoubtedly face a flat someday.

Almost all punctures occur in the rear because of the greater weight that tire supports and because it is the drive wheel. The following is therefore rear-tire repair, but all directions apply to the front tire except, of course, those involving components not located up front.

First, shift the chain onto the smallest freewheel cog to assist in wheel removal. Next, disengage the rear brake so as to spread the brake pads from the rim sufficiently to let the tire pass between them. (When engaged, the pads of properly adjusted brakes sit very close to the rim—too close to allow for wheel removal.)

And how do you disengage the brake? If you have cantilever or U-brakes you should be able to reach under the rim (between the

• **Cantilever brake being released
for wheel removal** •

spokes), squeeze the pads toward each other, grab hold of the
small knob at the end of the brake cable, and lift it free. With some
cantilevers it is possible to do this by reaching over the wheel. If
your brakes are powercam, squeeze the pads together as before
and twist the cam (the X-shaped metal plate between both brake
arms) free.

If your brake cable is too tight for you to release the pads in this
manner, you have two options. (Well, really three, but who wants to
walk home?) You can release brake cable tension by screwing the
brake cable adjustment barrel (usually found by the handlebar
brake lever) toward the brake lever. Or you can use your crescent
or allen wrench to remove one brake pad.

• Roller cam brake •

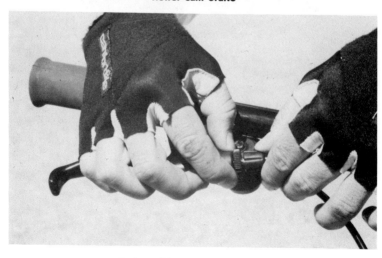

• Brake cable adjustment barrel •

• **Quick-release lever** •

Now you can remove the wheel. Flip the bike on its back or side, trip the quick-release lever or loosen the wheel axle nuts, and, taking hold of the derailleur body, pull it back toward you (thus moving the upper jockey pulley away from the freewheel cogs).

Wheels often become stuck in their dropouts (that portion of the frame that holds the wheel axles) and may require a sharp rap with the heel of the hand near the top of the tire to dislodge them.

When you have lifted the wheel free from the frame, let all remaining air out of the tube. You will probably have Schrader valves on your bike (the automobile-type valves); the air is released by depressing the tiny metal shaft in the center of the round valve. If yours is a Presta valve, unscrew the round top a few turns (counterclockwise), then depress it. Now take the non-hook end (usually the lesser-angled end) of one tire lever and, beveled side up, work it underneath the bead. (Begin working with this first lever at a point

• **Derailleur body being pulled back
for wheel removal.** •

on the wheel *opposite* the valve stem.) Push down (toward the spokes) on the tire lever in your hand. Hook the slotted lever side onto a spoke to hold it and the tire in place (notice earlier drawing). This frees both hands for the next step.

With the second lever, work the tip beneath the tire bead about an inch or so from the first lever. Again, push down to pop the bead away from its seat in the rim. If you can't do this, move the second tire lever slightly closer to the first. Now continue to work the bead away from the rim all around the wheel, until one side of the tire is complete-ly free.

At this point I begin working one of the spoons (another name for tire levers) from the opposite side of the wheel, manipulating the second bead off the rim. (You are now working the bead off the rim *away* from you in direction because both beads must come off the same side to free the tire.) Taking one side of the tire off at a time is much easier than trying to force both beads off at once. Expect a new tire to be more difficult to remove than an old one. However, ATB tires are much easier to peel off than racing or thin-tire touring rubber, old or new.

Some riders, however, including Ed Chauner and my two mechanics Ken and Brad, prefer not to remove this second beading, allowing the tire to remain on the rim and simply extracting the tube. This is not done primarily to save time, they all told me, but instead to allow for tube/tire orientation that, in the case of extremely slow leaks, tells the rider where to search his tube once the culprit tack or cactus thorn has been found in the casing. (Come to think of it, this would also keep you from remounting today's "directional" tires incorrectly. Look on your sidewall for arrows that indicate proper tire direction, because some come with tread intended to run one way only.)

My personal method of finding such protrusions is to overlap my fingers inside the casing and spin them around the circumference of the tire, but a particular drawback should be noted. I have, on occasion, run a finger into a thorn or shard of glass a bit too quickly. Remember to make your search slowly.

The mechanics also stated that the *kind* of hole in the tube should be seen as a diagnostic tool (albeit a rather crude one) hinting at what caused the flat. A single hole is usually caused by something coming through the tire casing; a "snakebite" hole (actually two tiny holes, side by side) is the result of "rim pinch"—where underinflation or tremendous force has caused the wheel rim to pinch the tube against an object. In the latter case you will not, of course, find anything puncturing the tire wall.

With the tube out of the tire, inflate it until it is firm and somewhat fat, but (in Ken's words) "not so that it looks like a bloated snake. You run a chance of blowing it up." Now listen for escaping air. Only twice in my life have I had to hold a tube under water to find a pinprick hole by following escaping air bubbles to the source. And only *once* in a quarter century of serious pedaling have I found the extremely slow leak to be the result of a valve core. (If your tube has a Schrader valve, be sure the air is not escaping from the threaded center valve core. If this core is not screwed tightly into these threads an air leak will result. The proper tool to tighten a valve core is the valve cover tool, a tiny slotted metal cap you should buy to replace the worthless black plastic caps present on all the tubes sold.)

• **Ken listening for air escaping from tube.
Notice air stream from left ear.** •

There was a time when I drew a tight circle around holes with a ballpoint pen. Although I cannot recall this ever causing problems, Brad and Ken explained what I should have thought of long ago: Ink can cause a patch to fail to adhere around the edges if you don't rough up the tube beyond the inked circle. To mark a tiny hole they too use ballpoints, but instead of a circle they draw three arrows pointing toward the site, ending them more than a patch-length distant.

When the hole is located and marked, let all the air out (you don't want any blowing out the hole while you're applying the patch) and rough up the area—in one direction only—with the patch-kit scraper. Be sure to do a good job of it, short of putting additional holes in the tube, and be sure to roughen an area a bit larger than the size of the patch.

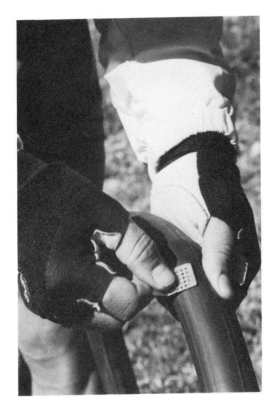

• **Roughing the tube** •

Apply the glue—a bit more glue than necessary to cover the patch area—with a somewhat-clean finger. Most kits suggest waiting until the glue is dry to apply the patch—so wait. Hurry this step and there's a good chance you'll be taking the wheel off the bike again a few miles down the road. Be careful not to touch the patch side that goes on the tube and, beginning at patch center and running toward the edges, press the patch with a spoon or the rounded end of another tool. In this manner you will drive out any remaining air bubbles.

When the patch appears to be holding well along the edges, pump a very slight amount of air into the tube to avoid wrinkles when it's placed back inside the tire. Put the tube in the tire (Ken and Brad suggest "dusting" the top of the patch with dirt—unless you happen

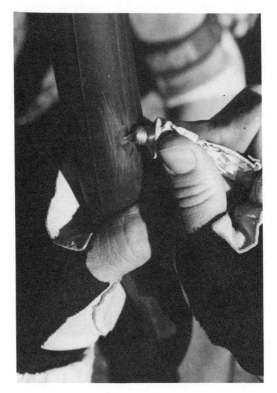

• **Applying glue to the hole** •

to have talc with you—to keep the patch from adhering to the tire casing in the future), then push the valve stem through the valve-stem hole in the rim and reseat one of the beads (using a tire lever with the beveled side down). Once one side of the tire—one bead—is back in place, begin reseating the second bead. (Removing all air at this point reduces the chance of puncture with the tire lever.) In taking off a tire you begin *opposite* the stem; in replacing it you begin work at the stem and work away from it in both directions, being sure to keep the stem pointing straight up. Riders who fail to do this, or who ride with low air pressure in their tires (which causes the tube to shift and the valve stem to angle out of the hole), cause wearing of the stem along its side and base. Once a hole occurs in the valve stem the entire tube is shot, because stems can't hold a patch.

• **Peeling away backing from the patch** •

With new thin tires I can usually restore by hand all the second bead except for about six inches before resorting to a spoon. But this second bead of ATB tires, especially after their first time off and on the rim, can sometimes be reinstalled without any tools at all.

I must admit to being surprised when Ken and Brad pumped in perhaps ten psi, then spent a solid minute inspecting both sides of the rim for "tube pinch"—the presence of the tube between the rim and tire bead. They did this by peeling back the bead slightly and looking for the tube peeking underneath. I explained that I had never had this problem, but both of them had, and it is, of course, fatal once full air pressure is restored. You also have to be especially careful of this when blowing up a tire with a carbon-dioxide cartridge or at a filling station. If you do have a pinched tube, let all the air out and work the tube back (carefully!) under the bead with a spoon. Preferable to this, if you can manage it, is to make the tube slip back up inside the tire casing by rocking the tire backward at the point of tube pinch, thereby lifting the tire bead slightly. Or take the tire completely off and start afresh.

If both beads are properly seated and the stem is still perpendicular, inflate the tire to desired pressure (doing so before restoring it to the bike frame saves one step in case you've goofed with the patch; inexpensive tires on cheap rims, I am told, can sometimes unseat themselves during reinflation) and restore the wheel to the frame. Do so by once again pulling the derailleur cage back toward you and out of the way, then dropping the smallest freewheel cog into the chain and settling the axle into the dropouts. Look down the back of the tire toward the bottom bracket (the point where chainstays and seat tube meet) to center the wheel. More expensive bikes will center it automatically when you pull the axle back to the dropout "stops." Close the quick-release lever or tighten the axle nuts, *restore your rear brake to working order,* and take off.

But first, a word on the quick release. It is *not* a nut with a handle. If it is properly set you should begin encountering stiffness on the lever when closing it to a half-mast position or slightly farther. It should not be so difficult to close that it requires pounding, and having to grip the seatstay with the fingers while depressing the quick-release lever with the heel of that hand will leave the lever parallel to the seatstay tube—an extremely difficult position for opening the lever the next time you need to remove your wheel. If you find that pounding or gripping the frame tube is necessary to close the lever, back it off (make it easier to close) by loosening the bale nut on the other side of the frame.

DERAILLEUR ADJUSTMENT

Major adjustments of the derailleurs are seldom required out on the trail, so the following instructions do not include movement of high and low gear adjusting screws. Nor are broken cables common, as they are on thin-tire bikes, because ATBs employ nearly indestructible cables of a gauge once seen only on motorcycles.

In fact, the only time trail riders ever seem to work on their gears is (1) when mud or sand has forced a long-delayed cleaning, and (2) when the chain makes noise after gear shifts.

• **Gear cable adjustment barrel** •

If your chain is making noise after shifting gears, the derailleur probably has failed to place the chain exactly on the desired sprocket. First try moving the shift lever slightly in each direction. If this does not make the noise go away you should adjust the tension in the gear cable. Have someone hold up the back of your bike while you pedal with one hand and adjust the barrel with the other. You will both feel and hear when the chain is centered properly over the sprocket.

CHAIN REPAIR

Few riders ever experience a broken chain. Some riders will develop frozen links. But all riders will someday have a chain badly in need of cleaning. Heed, therefore, those parts of the following that pertain to your riding needs.

We'll begin with frozen and broken links, because a mountain biker in the backcountry with such a problem—and without tools or without the knowledge to right it himself—is a sorry sight to behold. This repair requires a chain rivet tool (also called simply a chain tool).

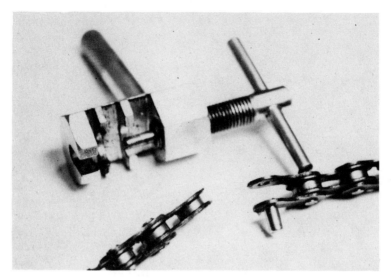

· Chain tool with disconnected chain ·

When a link becomes frozen (a condition most often caused by insufficient lubrication) it makes itself known by jumping over teeth in the sprockets or by causing the rear derailleur to jerk forward suddenly as it passes over the jockey and tension pulleys. Elevate your rear wheel and turn the crank to find the culprit link; when you do, coat it with a light oil (if you have been using oil as lubrication, that is) and work the link side to side (the opposite direction of its normal movement) with your fingers. This may free it. If not, you'll have to employ the chain tool.

This tool, when viewed from the side, looks like a wide U, with two shorter "walls" of metal between. Place the tool in front of you with the handle to the right side. Twist the handle counterclockwise to remove the rivet pin (see photo) from view. Now take the chain and place it over the first of these inner walls from the right side. (It will usually be somewhat wider than the left-hand wall.) Notice, when you view your chain tool from the top, that these walls have an open space in the middle that the chain roller rests in, with the "plates" on either side of the wall. (Look at an individual link. Each is made up of these metal side plates, small round bars called "rollers" to engage the teeth of the sprockets, and tiny rivets to hold the side plates and rollers together.)

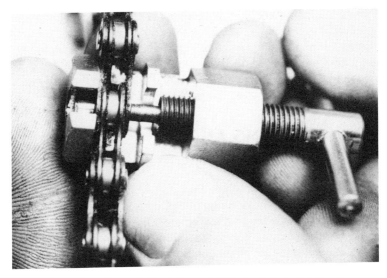

• **Chain tool on chain; both chain and chain tool rivet pins in view.** •

To free a frozen link, place it as described above on the right-hand wall of the chain rivet tool. Turn the tool handle clockwise until the tool rivet pin touches the chain rivet. As you turn the handle more, notice how the plates move slightly farther apart. Most often only the slightest rivet adjustment is necessary to free the link. Be sure not to push the chain rivet flush with the side plate; its length is such that it should extend slightly past the plates on both sides. If it is necessary to push the rivet flush to free the link, simply turn the chain over in the tool and apply pressure against the opposite end of the rivet.

In the case of a chain break, a spare link and chain tool in your kit allows you to remove the broken link completely and replace it with a spare. This requires that the chain rivet be driven out of one side plate past the roller, yet still remain in place in the far side plate. (I *know* this sounds very confusing. But it won't be when you're attempting the repair.) Keeping the rivet in the far side plate can be a little tricky at first, so I suggest you run through this procedure a couple of times before you try it on the trail. Bike shops will often have lengths of old chains with which you can practice.

Place the chain over the left-hand wall of your chain tool and turn the handle clockwise until the tool rivet pin touches the chain rivet.

Then continue turning very carefully until the roller can be pulled free, but with the chain rivet still in the far side plate. Install the new link by turning the chain tool around and driving the chain rivet through the new roller and side plate. You'll probably find that it's frozen when replaced. If so, simply place this link on the right-hand plate and free it, following the directions above.

CHAIN CLEANING AND LUBRICATION

In the past few years a number of commercial brush-and-solvent-type chain cleaners have entered the market. If used often these will do a fair job of removing a large part of road grime. But there will come a time when the old procedure of complete chain removal, a good dunking in a coffee can of white gas (or other solvent), and a frontal attack with a toothbrush is required. I then hang mine to drip dry, rub it with a cloth, clean all chain contact points on the bike (chainwheels, cogs, derailleur pulleys), and reinstall.

Because I am most often on dirt and pavement (relatively seldom on sand), and because I prefer a small bottle of oil in my panniers to an aerosol can, I choose against both paraffin and sprays for lubrication. My practice is simply to use a single drop of oil on each roller, spin the chain a few times, let it sit for a while, then wipe almost dry with a cloth.

However, a friend of mine who rides the sands of southern Utah quite often, and another who rides primarily in dirt, swear by paraffin. Their arguments are, of course, a cleaner bike and less wear and tear on the chain and all its contact points (which they attribute to dirt not being attracted to—and held in place by—an oily, greasy chain). Yet when I asked Brad and Ken their opinions of paraffin, their response was a single word: "dinosaur."

I begged them to expound, and they told me how they had tested paraffin's efficiency by adding oil to the paraffined chain of a bike they were pedaling on a tune-up stand. The cyclic rate increased dramatically. The mechanics agree that wax does not attract dirt, but teflon-based lubricants that go to a dry rather than wet finish, they say, are almost as good at repelling dirt and sand and do a better job of lubrication. *And* they're much easier to apply.

• **An ounce of prevention . . .** •

APPENDIX A:
GEAR CHART FOR 26-INCH WHEEL

APPENDIX A: *Gear Chart for 26" Wheel*

Number of teeth in front sprocket

	24	26	28	30	32	34	36	38	40	42	44	46	48	50	52
12	52	56.3	60.7	65	69.3	73.4	78	82.3	86.7	91	95.3	99.7	104	108.3	112.7
13	48	52	56	60	64	68	72	76	80	84	88	92	96	100	104
14	44.6	48.3	52	55.8	59.4	63.1	66.9	70.6	74.3	78	81.7	85.4	89.1	92.9	96.6
15	41.6	45.1	48.5	52	55.5	58.9	62.4	65.9	69.3	72.8	76.3	79.7	83.2	86.7	90.1
16	39	42.3	45.5	48.8	52	55.3	58.5	61.8	65	68.3	71.5	74.8	78	81.3	84.5
17	36.7	39.8	42.8	45.9	48.9	52	55.1	58.1	61.2	64.2	67.3	70.4	73.4	76.5	79.5
18	34.7	37.6	40.4	43.3	46.2	49.1	52	54.9	57.8	60.7	63.6	66.4	69.3	72.2	75.1
19	32.8	35.6	38.3	41.1	43.8	46.5	49.3	52	54.7	57.8	60.2	62.9	65.7	68.4	71.2
20	31.2	33.8	36.4	39	41.6	44.2	46.8	49.4	52	54.6	57.2	59.8	62.4	65	67.6
21	29.7	32.2	34.7	37.1	39.6	42.1	44.6	47	49.5	52	54.5	57	59.4	61.9	63.4
22	28.4	30.7	33.1	35.5	37.8	40.2	42.5	44.9	47.3	49.6	52	54.4	56.7	59.1	61.5
23	27.1	29.4	31.7	33.9	36.2	38.4	40.7	43	45.2	47.5	49.7	52	54.3	56.5	58.8
24	26	28.2	30.3	32.5	34.7	36.8	39	41.2	43.3	45.5	47.7	49.8	52	54.2	56.3
25	25	27	29.1	31.2	33.3	35.4	37.4	39.5	41.6	43.7	45.8	47.8	49.9	52	54.1
26	24	26	28	30	32	34	36	38	40	42	44	46	48	50	52
27	23.1	25	27	28.9	30.8	32.7	34.7	36.6	38.5	40.4	42.4	44.3	46.2	48.1	50.1
28	22.3	24.1	26	27.9	29.7	31.6	33.4	35.3	37.1	39	40.9	42.7	44.6	46.4	48.3
29	21.5	23.3	25.1	26.9	28.7	30.5	32.3	34.1	35.9	37.7	39.4	41.2	43	44.8	46.6
30	20.8	22.5	24.3	26	27.7	29.5	31.2	32.9	34.7	36.4	38.1	39.9	41.6	43.3	45.1
31	20.1	21.8	23.5	25.2	26.8	28.5	30.2	31.9	33.5	35.2	36.9	38.6	40.3	41.9	43.6
32	19.5	21.1	22.8	24.4	26	27.6	29.3	30.9	32.5	34.1	35.8	37.4	39	40.6	42.3
33	18.9	20.5	22.1	23.6	25.2	26.7	28.4	29.9	31.5	33.1	34.7	36.2	37.8	39.4	41
34	18.4	19.9	21.4	22.9	24.5	26	27.5	29.1	30.6	32.1	33.6	35.2	36.7	38.2	39.8
35	17.8	19.3	20.8	22.3	23.8	25.3	26.7	28.2	29.7	31.2	32.7	34.2	35.7	37.1	38.6
36	17.3	18.8	20.2	21.7	23.1	24.6	26	27.4	28.9	30.3	31.8	33.2	34.7	36.1	37.6

(The leftmost column is labeled vertically: Number of teeth in rear sprocket)

$$\text{inch gear} = \frac{\text{\# teeth in front sprocket}}{\text{\# teeth in rear sprocket}} \times \text{wheel diameter in inches}$$

Example: $\frac{48}{13} \times 26 = 96$ inch gear

(Compute linear distance traveled with each crank rotation by multiplying "inch gear" by pi = 3.14)

Example: $96 \times 3.14 = 301.44"$ (or 25.12′ linear distance)

APPENDIX B:
MOUNTAIN BIKE TOURING COMPANIES

Acomplete list of bicycle touring companies that include off-road tours would require several pages; you will find names and addresses in the back pages of most cycling magazines. The following are companies I've toured with, plus a few I've not yet had the chance to sample but have heard good reports about from those who have.

BACKCOUNTRY
P.O. Box 4029
Bozeman, MT 59772
(406) 586-3556

BACKROADS BICYCLE TOURING
1516 Fifth Street
Berkeley, CA 94710
(800) 533-2573

KAIBAB BIKE TOURS
391 South Main
Moab, UT 84532
(800) 451-1133

RIM TOURS
94 West 1st North
Moab, UT 84532
(801) 259-5223

TIMBERLINE BICYCLE TOURS
3261 Oneida Way
Denver, CO 80224
(303) 759-3804

VERMONT BICYCLE TOURING
Box 711
Bristol, VT 05443
(802) 453-4811

WESTERN SPIRIT CYCLING
P.O. Box 411
Moab, UT 84532
(800) 845-BIKE
(801) 259-8732

Progressive Travels does not at this time offer rides specifically for mountain bikers, but I've toured with them recently and can suggest that if you have a desire to see the Pacific Northwest—in great style and at a pace that allows you time to cover the day's paved route and still lets you bike off-road to your heart's content (on good dirt roads, that is; Progressive's hybrid bikes aren't built for tough trails)—give them a call:

PROGRESSIVE TRAVELS
1932 First Avenue, Suite 1100
Seattle, WA 98101
(800) 245-2229
(206) 443-4228 (fax)

APPENDIX C:
ED CHAUNER'S RIDING SCHOOL

You've now read about Ed's mountain bike class. But if you'd like to hone your skills directly under his watchful eye, plus add the thrill of putting your bike aboard a tram that takes you to an eleven-thousand-foot peak high in the Rockies (how's *that* for great climbing technique?) and enjoy a great descent, contact:

SNOWBIRD SKI AND SUMMER RESORT
Snowbird, UT 84092
(801) 742-2222
521-6040 (from Salt Lake)
(801) 742-2150 (fax)

GLOSSARY

This short list does not contain all the words used by mountain bike enthusiasts when discussing their sport, but it should be sufficient as an introduction to the lingua franca you'll hear on the trails.

ATB. All-terrain bike. This, like "fat-tire bike," is another name for a mountain bike.

ATV. All-terrain vehicle. This usually refers to the loud, fume-spewing three- or four-wheeled motorized vehicles you will not enjoy meeting on the trail—except, of course, if you crash and have to hitch a ride out on one.

bladed. Refers to a dirt road that has been smoothed out by the use of a wide blade on earth-moving equipment; blading gets rid of the teeth-chattering, much-cursed washboards found on so many dirt roads after heavy vehicle use.

blaze. A mark on a tree made by chipping away a piece of the bark, usually done to designate a trail; such trails are sometimes described as blazed.

BLM. Bureau of Land Management, an agency of the federal government.

clean. Although this can be used to describe what you and your bike *won't* be after following most trails, the term is most often used as a verb to denote the action of pedaling a tough section of trail successfully.

deadfall. A tangled mass of fallen trees or branches.

diversion ditch. A usually narrow, shallow ditch dug across or around a trail; funneling the water in this manner keeps it from destroying the trail.

double-track. The dual tracks made by a jeep or other vehicle, with grass, weeds, or rocks between; the mountain biker can therefore ride in either of the tracks, but will find that whichever he chooses, and no matter how many times he changes back and forth, the other track will appear to offer smoother travel.

dugway. A steep, unpaved, switchbacked descent.

feathering. Using a light touch on the brake lever, hitting it lightly many times rather than very hard or locking the brake.

four-wheel-drive. Any vehicle with drive-wheel capability on all four wheels (a jeep, for instance, as compared with a two-wheel-drive passenger car), or a rough road or trail that requires four-wheel-drive capability to traverse it.

game trail. The usually narrow trail made by deer, elk, or other game.

gated. A gated trail simply has a gate across it; don't forget that the rule is if you find a gate closed, close it behind you; if you find one open, leave it that way.

Giardia. Shorthand for *Giardia lamblia*, and known as the "backpacker's bane" until we mountain bikers expropriated it. This is a waterborne parasite that begins its life cycle when swallowed, and one to four weeks later has its host bloated, vomiting, shivering with chills, and living in the bathroom. The disease can be avoided by treating (purifying) the water acquired along the trail.

gnarly. A terribly unpoetic term, thankfully used less and less these days; it refers to very tough trails.

hardpack. Used to describe a trail in which the dirt surface is packed down hard; such trails make for good and fast riding and very painful landings. Bikers most often use "hardpack" as both a noun and adjective, and "hardpacked" as an adjective only (the grammar lesson will help you when diagramming sentences in camp).

headplant. A dive over the handlebars, usually accompanied by the bike flipping up and over you.

jeep road, jeep trail. A rough road or trail that requires four-wheel-drive capability (or a horse or mountain bike) to traverse it.

kamikaze. Although this once referred primarily to those Japanese fliers who quaffed a glass of sake, then flew off as human bombs in suicide missions against U.S. naval vessels, it more recently has been applied to the idiot mountain bikers who far less honorably scream down hiking trails, endangering the physical and mental safety of the walking, jogging, biking, and equestrian traffic they meet. Deck guns were necessary to stop the Japanese kamikaze pilots, but a bike pump or walking staff in the spokes is sufficient for the current-day kamikazes who threaten to get us all kicked off the trails.

multipurpose. A BLM designation of land that is open to multipurpose use; mountain bikers are allowed.

out-and-back. A ride in which you will return on the same trail you pedaled out; although this might sound far more boring than a loop route, many trails look very different when pedaled in the opposite direction.

portage. To carry your bike on your person.

quads. Bikers use this term to refer both to the extensor muscle in the front part of the thigh (which is separated into four parts), and to USGS maps. The expression "Nice quads!" always refers to the former, however, except in those instances when the speaker is an engineer.

runoff. Rainwater or snowmelt.

signed. A signed trail is denoted by signs in place of blazes.

single-track. A single track through grass or brush or over rocky terrain, often created by deer, elk, or backpackers; single-track riding is some of the best fun around.

slickrock. Rock-hard, compacted sandstone that is *great* to ride and even prettier to look at; you'll appreciate it more if you think of it as a petrified sand dune or seabed, and if the rider before you hasn't left tire marks (through unnecessary skidding) or granola bar wrappers behind.

snowmelt. Runoff produced by the melting of snow.

snowpack. Unmelted snow accumulated over weeks or months of winter, or over years in high mountain terrain.

spur. A road or trail that intersects the main trail you're following.

technical. Terrain that is difficult to ride due not to its grade (steepness) but because of obstacles—rocks, logs, ledges, loose soil, etc.

topo. Short for topographical map, the kind that shows both linear distance *and* elevation gain and loss. Topo is pronounced with both vowels long.

two-wheel-drive. Any vehicle with drive-wheel capability on only two wheels (a passenger car, for instance, compared with a jeep), or an easy road or trail that a two-wheel-drive vehicle can traverse.

washboard. A road with many ridges spaced closely together, like the ripples on a washboard; these make for very rough riding and even worse driving in a car or jeep.

waterbar. Earth, rock, or wooden structures that funnel water off trails.

wilderness area. Land that is officially set aside by the federal government to remain *natural* —pure, pristine, and untrammeled by any vehicle, including mountain bikes. Though mountain bikes had not been born in 1964 (when the U.S. Congress passed the Wilderness Act, thereby establishing the National Wilderness Preservation System), they are considered a "form of mechanical transport" and are thereby excluded; in short, stay out.

GLOSSARY

wind chill. A reference to the wind's cooling effect on exposed flesh; for example, if the temperature is 10 degrees Fahrenheit and the wind is blowing at 20 miles per hour, the wind-chill effect (that is, the actual temperature to which your skin reacts) is *minus* 32 degrees; if you are riding in wet conditions things are even worse, because the wind-chill effect would then be minus 74 degrees! Remember too that you increase wind speed, and therefore wind-chill effect, by the speed at which you are pedaling.

windfall. Anything (trees, limbs, brush) blown down by the wind.

INDEX